Our Autistic Life

The Poetry of Autistic Spectrum Autists

Rena and Mike Mortenson

Parson's Porch Books

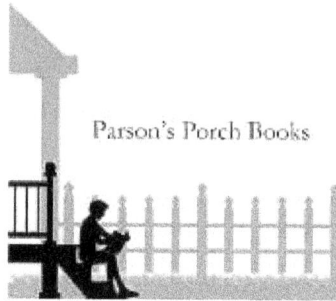

Our Autistic Life: The Poetry of Autistic Spectrum Autists
ISBN: Softcover 978-1-960326-10-2

Copyright © 2022 by Rena and Mike Mortenson

Parson's Porch Books is an imprint of Parson's Porch *&* Company (PP*&*C) in Cleveland, Tennessee. PP*&*C is a self-funded charity which earns money by publishing books of noted authors, representing all genres. Its face and voice is **David Russell Tullock** (dtullock@parsonsporch.com).

Parson's Porch *&* Company *turns books into bread & milk* by sharing its profits with the poor.

www.parsonsporch.com

Our Autistic Life

Dedication

We would like to dedicate this book to our family and friends who over the years have helped us tremendously as we have taken our autistic journey. We also dedicate this book to all of those of you who have worked with autistics in the past and know the challenges that we face every day just to get by. Lastly, we dedicate this book to those of you who are neurologically typical and do not live on the autistic spectrum in hopes that you can learn from the lessons in this book as well.

Contents

Dedication 5

Introduction 9

Foreword 11

Belittle Be Not 15

Through the Eyes of a Child 17

Appointments 19

Not Everything is What it Seems..21

Living on the spectrum...23

I Wonder..28

I am I Said..30

The Empty Chair 34

Betrayal..38

Letting Go 39

Timber's Whispering Wind...40

The Power of the Rain 41

Haiku 43

The Bully..47

Elderly Eyes..49

The Brown Things 51

Give it your All 54

Be the Storm 56

What Kind of People are We?..59

You Must Learn to Dance in the Rain......................................61

Work in Progress 64

Just a Little Sick Humor 66

Chocolate 70

Deep in Thought 72

Unseasonably Cold...74

Real True Love..76

Flowers Come Back 78

Broken...80

Only My Way 83

My Man 86

Wood Ticks, Mosquitos and Gnats 89

Wicked Twister 91

Don't Mess With Me 93

Is it All Really Worth it? 96

Neurologically Typical Verses Autistic 98

My Daddy 101
True Friends 104
Eat a Treat 106
Our Fur Kids Come First 108
Our Beautiful Property 110
Life in the Wetland 114
Earthly Power 117
Vermin 119
A Beautiful Place 122
An Animal's Point of View 123
Parents 124
Children 125
My Beautiful Creature 126
Tree Love 128
Open Letter to a friend 130

Introduction

Both the authors of this book, Mike and Rena Mortenson, who have been married for over 40 years, are on the autistic spectrum and although they are considered high functioning, their day-to-day survival can often be extremely hard and draining just to get by. One of their most favorite things to do is taking in abused, abandoned, and rejected dogs and cats to give them a safe and wonderful place to live. Mike and Rena are extremely gifted in writing poetry about their day-to-day trials and tribulations. The poems contained in this book come from actual experiences and thoughts they have had over the span of their lives. This collection of the poems tells stories of their life challenges, hardships, and missteps. These poems come directly from their hearts and shows the wisdom they have learned over their lifetimes. Some poems are funny, some sad, some crazy, but yet all contain lessons that are designed to improve the lives of other autistics as well as provide great narrative for teachers, therapists, parents, as well as other people who may be close to the life of an autistic. Enjoy.

- Mike Green, Editor & Project Manager

Foreword

I am an Autistic adult woman on the Autism Spectrum who has been down a lot of rocky roads during my lifetime. I have faced a lot of struggles that often had become more than I could handle, and I am proudly still here to tell my story.

Autism is a neurological disorder of a person's brain wiring. Many connections in our brain wiring are either quite different from the typical person or some of it isn't there at all. Autism is not curable and is with us at birth and remains with us until we depart this earth. Autistic people have deficits that other neurologically typical people have very little understanding of. We see things through a very different thought process and have difficulty recognizing what typical people are often trying to say. I can explain it simply by saying we are a different operating system. Our minds process information completely in a different way from how the usual mind works. We are prone to anxiety and depression which makes our lives a lot more difficult than the ordinary person. It often affects our stomach.

Being Autistic myself, I have had many vast experiences that come to mind. Times when I was so afraid to allow others in because of the fear of rejection. My experience with the neurologically typical world, is that most of those people have a very hard time relating to us because our thought process often makes no sense to them. The typical world in my eyes, fears what they don't understand.

Because of my many struggles with relationships I am often less likely to engage in group activities for that very reason. Being misunderstood puts me out of my comfort zone. My therapist describes me as 'A PUSH AND PULL' type of person. Because I fear rejection, with one hand I pull people towards me, and then with the other hand I push them away. For me, that is a protection mechanism for survival in the typical world.

Often, I have had encounters with neurologically typical people who have not treated me as an equal. Because I'm different, they often consider me less of a person and I was relentlessly picked on as a child. That treatment has even moved into my adulthood in many cases.

I am very intelligent and often am way ahead of others in my realization of worldly issues but somehow, I am not seen as the intelligent and capable person I really am. Although I struggle to fit into the mold of the typical world, I am very aware of what is going on. It is like being in a bubble where others keep me safely tucked away from their interactions because they don't understand me, or people like me. This causes much frustration but also sends us autistic people into our own safe world.

There is a spectrum. Autistic people vary in their abilities and coping skills. I have often been referred to as high functioning, although if a person were to ask many neurologically typical people who have been in my life what they thought of me, they would report that I am a bit more moderate to low functioning much of the time in certain situations. My intentions are very often taken in the wrong light. Because I process things in such a different way, people more often don't see how intelligent I really am, or just how much I truly know

Being on the Autism Spectrum, I engage in many unusual activities that others perceive as odd. I am often seen spending loads of time in the presence of my rescue animals rather than among people. I also do a lot of things alone because it's just too hard for me to handle day to day interaction with groups of people who seem to judge me. I live in protection mode most of my waking moments. I take harsh judgement very hard and become hurt and emotionally damaged by other peer's abuse. Sadly, I feel I am damaged goods in many ways because of it and have not experienced the kind of support and acceptance I have always dreamed of. My hope is that this bridge between Autistic people and the rest of the world can become easier with more information and learning tools.

My talents lie in my ability to relate to animals and my rescue work gives me a purpose that to me is basically the main reason I don't give up on life completely when times get rough. I understand animal kind and they understand me. That is one time when I feel secure that I am considered very important and needed.

I also have a gift with animals and can bring abused and abandon animals back to trusting and loving companions. I have taken on many very serious cases during my lifetime where either an animal (mostly dogs and cats) have been badly broken and it took a relentless amount of attention and love to bring these companions back to health, or they had temperament problems, which of course being autistic I understand because I've lived it. I have taken animals into my loving home that have been both physically damaged or have special needs due to health issues that no one else wanted to deal with. Many of these animals are terribly afraid of people because they have been abused and injured in the process. Many folks out in the neurologically typical world have a lack of understanding when it comes to animals with special needs, or they don't have the desire to spend that quality of time working with what most of the world would consider rejects.

I myself having been treated in a similar way my entire life, do understand what these animals have been through, and I know how to reach out to them and make their lives better. This is a skill I have that no one can deny. Animals have given me love and acceptance in an otherwise very difficult world. They have given me a purpose.

I present to you, stories I tell from my heart through my poetry. Being a young person during my school years, CREATIVE WRITING was the only class I ever excelled at. I have always been well equipped when it came to expressing myself through my writing. My poetry tells the stories I never have the chance to share with others. I hope it can be a learning tool for folks who would enjoy getting a better understanding of what living on the autism spectrum entails.

Thank You
Rena Linda Kay Mortenson

Belittle Be Not

A small character in a person
is pronounced by their judgement of others,
to believe they're above
all their sisters and brothers.

Being willing to condemn
is the way some people act,
and is not fair at all
without even one fact.

Passing judgement so harsh
to any stranger you never knew,
while purposely hurting them
gives them a reason to sue.

To defame a person's character
without any real proof,
shows all others you're arrogant
and very aloof.

The world is a confusing
and difficult place,
the good a person has done
false statements will erase.

People who tell lies
to hurt without reason,
are committing something serious
like an act of treason.

That good person may have intentions
well-meaning in their heart,
they make the great effort
while hate will tear them apart.

It's hard to understand
what motivates a person to lie,
and cause damage to another
why bother to try.

If you destroy someone innocent
with your meaningless hate,
it will be useless to later be sorry
and is often too late.

To practice to live and let live
is a very simple trait,
no one is superior enough
to decide someone's fate.

It's hard to know exactly
what another person goes through,
and to try to ruin a life
is what lying will do.

Still there is a God
and it really won't be too long,
before those who do evil
will pay for their wrong.

God always knows the truth
no matter the size of a lie,
you won't tarnish my reputation
so don't even try.

With our Lord God
karma will be served,
and all of you liars
get what you deserve.

When the end comes to pass
all your lies will fade away,
you will have accomplished nothing
it doesn't matter what you say.

Learn the meaning of these words
belittle be not,
the truth will prevail
and you will be caught.

Through the Eyes of a Child

Wide innocent eyes
scanning the scene,
not a bone in their body
wants to be mean.

They look at their family
with love and hope,
because they are the one's
who teach them to cope.

Adults are their hero's
mom and dad are number one,
they enjoy even the little things
and cherish the fun.

When the weather is bad
their creative little brain,
even enjoys going outside
to play in the rain.

They feel unstoppable
nothing keeps them down,
their laughter is joyous
just a fun-loving sound.

A child doesn't see
the world in a skeptical light,
they see things all fresh
everything is alright.

When dandelions emerge
and are just a weed,
children see beauty
as something we need.

They see bright yellow flowers
and collect them with pride,
give them to their mothers
with smiles big and wide.

It's funny how an adult
worries about their lawn,
a dandelion is no longer pretty
that fresh feeling is gone.

A child sees all in the world
as an opportunity to learn,
they don't sweat the small stuff
there is no real concern.

So, try to keep the child
alive in your soul,
don't let things sour
make that your goal.

So full of life and happiness
is that young precious child,
they are the reason
we have all smiled.

Let the stamina of a child
give you energy and drive,
this might be the only true way
for you to survive.

A child does something special,
in their own unique loving way,
they can lift you up from the darkness
by the things that they say.

Through the eyes of a child
you will be able to cope,
with life's disappointments
and always have hope.

(Inspired by the little people and my friend Katharina Mensink's love for her two little girls)

Appointments

We have so much to do
and want to do it right now,
but with all these appointments
we really don't know how.

We need to keep moving
and doing all that we can,
getting important things done
was always our plan.

Then comes the phone call
with the time and the date,
appointments are continual
everything else has to wait.

We missed an important guest
because we were gone again,
we have to reschedule
but don't know when.

We have appointments all week
one every single day,
getting anything else accomplished
there just is no way.

There really isn't enough time
for us to be at home,
or to go out somewhere
to shop or to roam.

We wanted to make plans
with our significant one,
but with all these appointments
we won't get that done!

A friend calls to inquire
what we're doing today,
but we have an appointment
and no time to play.

If I hear about another appointment
then we really must talk,
if the car isn't working
we might have to walk.

We have tasks to do on the house
and need one more supply,
but we're at an appointment
we really did try.

With any more appointments
I just cannot commit,
my life is scheduled
I might have to quit.

We have so much to do
and want to do it today,
cancel that appointment
is all I can say.

Not Everything is What it Seems

There are times in life
when we are misjudged,
and for those who know the truth
their accusers are begrudged.

It's always better practice
to think something carefully through,
and really be certain what you think
is really even true.

You might make the mistake
of thinking someone did a certain thing,
and you just don't realize
pain your accusation will bring.

There might be a very good reason
why something happens a certain way,
and when you become negative
a character is destroyed by what you say.

You may believe someone caused a problem
that was already preexisting,
you could ruin a good reputation
by falsely insisting.

In any given situation
you may not have all the facts,
you really will defile a character
with all your meaningless attacks.

Many times, a person you insult
may go above and beyond,
where they have developed trust
with a very special bond.

Then you step in with your lies
and disrupt all the work they have done,
you may fool some with your deceit
but you really haven't won.

Truth has a way of coming out
no matter how much you try,
to make a person look bad
with nothing but a lie.

Good people certainly will learn
what is really going on,
and when all is said and done
destructive efforts will be gone.

You might be vindictive
with an ax to grind,
but good folks will always see
you are just not kind.

When a person continually works
to expose someone else's flaw,
they will eventually be figured out
it is just the luck of the draw.

So just always keep in mind
no one listens to your screams,
they will see that you're a fake
not everything is what it seems.

Living on the spectrum

Living on the spectrum
I am an autistic adult,
my unusual brain wiring
actually, isn't my fault.

I was born this way
and live with this deficit,
judgmental people out there
are as cruel as they can get.

People tend to judge me
they separate me from the rest,
it doesn't matter to them
if I am doing my best.

I struggle for acceptance
every single day,
communication is difficult
no matter what I say.

I feel like I live with a sentence
and a label around my neck,
people are like a judge and jury
with the things they expect.

I just can't seem to win
no matter how hard I try,
no one seems to understand
and I never know the reason why.

I make extra special effort
to fit in their little box,
but as soon as I seem different
I cringe when someone talks.

I listen to accusations
and all the sarcastic hype,
I guess I fit in nowhere
I just am not their type.

Although friendship means a lot to me
it seems to always be out of reach,
I try to be liked
as I listen to them preach.

To hear that I'm not good enough
to be a part of any group,
I am constantly working hard
to jump through every hoop.

Life for me is stressful
always being accused all the time,
of doing something wrong
like I have committed a crime.

It doesn't seem to matter
that I have feelings too,
whenever I try to work things out
the problem only grew.

Then there is always a certain person
who will bully me really bad,
if I try to defend myself
I end up alone and really sad.

It is much easier
for others to place blame,
than it is to see the truth
and treat me just the same.

I have never been good enough
to be treated like an equal,
they just black ball me from the group
like waiting for their sequel.

They tell others not to include me
to never allow me another chance,
then I get ridiculed
if I dare to take a stance.

They always want the last word
I consider that so unfair,
when I see them anywhere
they will gossip and stare.

So I eventually end up alone
being left out of all the fun,
they feel good about themselves
no matter what they've done.

I try endlessly to be liked
and to be nothing but decent,
but because of discrimination
this hasn't been very recent.

I often keep to myself
and am forced to retreat,
I have a good reason to withdraw
with a feeling of defeat.

Autism often causes me
to be quite perturbed,
facing numerous difficulties
I never get what I deserve.

When the neurologically typical world
becomes very confused with us,
they decide to react violently
becoming combative and unjust.

A person on the autism spectrum
struggles with sensory overload,
but others think we're unstable
because that is what they're told.

In the true reality of things
we might just need a little space,
we sometimes take a time out
and do things at our own pace.

Regular people don't believe
that we should be allowed a break,
but at least they see what they get
and we are never fake.

Often times blunt honestly
is an autism trait,
we might tell it like it is
because we have a lot on our plate.

Autistic folks might even stem
which consists of body motion,
it has a calming affect for us
others have a different notion.

The autistic mind is complex
our feelings are intense,
the neurologically typical world
thinks we don't make any sense.

Those who are not on the spectrum
fear what they don't understand,
they want autistic folks
to do as they command.

Our minds operate quite differently
because of the wiring in our brain,
we are moving in another direction
like cars in another lane.

We will reach our destination
in our own sweet time,
being different is unique
it doesn't mean we're out of line.

Being autistic every day
is hard to say the least,
it is only your rejection
that brings out the beast.

We are not odd but only different
and others may see that as bad,
for those who judge us this way
that is truly sad.

Autistic folks have a perfect right
to coexist with all the rest,
just because a person is typical
they don't wear a metal on their chest.

When we're hurt or frustrated
we might have to vent,
with a bit of acceptance
these are things we can prevent.

Just like a person who can't walk
our disability is very real,
think about how you respond
and what it will reveal.

A meltdown may occur at difficult times
when autistic folks are pushed too hard,
the pain and rejection we have seen
has left us very scarred.

You must always remember
that life for you is typical,
autistic folks are often judged
and life for them is critical.

You might think you can change autism
is this really where you're at?
That idea is quite impossible
so good luck with that.

Living on the Autism spectrum
is how people like us have to live,
remember that how it all works out
depends upon what you are willing to give.

I Wonder

So often I wonder with great intent
if my mother looks down from above,
knowing that I miss her touch
and that I face loneliness without her love.

I wonder if Heaven's shelter
keeps her isolated from earthly pain,
and if she has forgotten those left behind
since she is now with my brother Wayne.

It comforts me very much to know
that my mom is reunited with her first-born son,
still, I wonder in my weakness
if I should have been the one.

My brother had a place here on earth
because he was always loved and understood,
while I have been a burden
and always felt I was no good.

My brother Wayne was popular
smart and so happy on this earth,
he was a special kind of angel
in Gods plan since the time of his birth.

When our Lord called my brother home
when he was only eight years old,
I kept thinking it should have been me
because I am weak, and he was so very bold.

I sit in the darkness of my room
staring through my window at the sky,
feeling abandon, confused and lost
as I hear myself begin to cry.

I want to feel my mother hold me
and melt away all this sorrow,
so, I can finally believe
in a much better tomorrow.

I wonder if God has made His plans
for me to come to Heaven one day,
so that I will have a forever home
where I know that I can stay.

I pray the day will come at last
when our Lord will sing my song,
as he welcomes me with open arms
to that safe place and I will always belong.

I am I Said

July came into season
in the summer of 1956,
a blue-eyed girl born
who everyone tried to fix.

This little child was different
from the very start,
her hands were always moving
with many emotions in her heart.

She lost her older brother to illness
at her raw age of only five,
she didn't really understand
what it meant to be alive.

It seemed the world was cruel
to this confused and lonely child,
she slipped away inside herself
with behaviors that were wild.

Watching her in action
could really tire people out,
as she ran from here to there
her thoughts were all about.

Not understanding death
she formed a deep dark place inside her,
a child who lost connection
who appeared to always be unsure.

Wayne went to live with God
were the words said by her mother,
all she understood was emptiness
from the loss of her older brother.

She played hard and long
was dirt from head to toe,
a true tom boy
and this began to show.

Her best friends were animal kind
dogs, cats, or another critter,
people frustrated her beyond compare
and only made her bitter.

A little child who had such admiration
for the brother she was forced to live without,
she became filled with anger
with that strong inner doubt.

Just as this troubled child
became old enough for school,
she was viewed to be withdrawn
and convinced that life was cruel.

Her mother knew there was something wrong
but didn't know how to help her,
whether there was more to all her struggles
her family was never sure.

During her beginning school experience
other kids began to tease,
it seemed to this little child
that it was impossible for her to please.

Peers became mean bullies
and were relentless with calling her names,
this child became fearful
and couldn't handle all their games.

She isolated herself quite often
and began to shut everyone out,
if forced to interact
This child would scream and shout.

She thought that her only option
was to try to make others afraid,
she couldn't go to her older brother
how she wished he could have stayed.

For a child with many fears
it was much easier to show that she was mad,
than it was to appear weak
and allow them to see her sad.

To bullies, a caring heart
is a sure damaging fate,
for a bully to know the effects
of all their appalling hate.

She had another sibling brother
and soon a baby girl would make two,
the baby being another girl
and happiness is all this baby ever knew.

The youngest of the family
came along to ease her parents pain,
but now her being the oldest told her
baby girl could never replace her brother Wayne.

Over all the years to come
this youngest sister was spoiled quite bad,
the oldest child who felt abandon these years
suffered and became even more sad.

Facing continual difficulty
became a burden that was great,
suffering was often a brutal reality
and seemed to be her fate.

Our July child one day became aware
of what made her different from her peers,
she was diagnosed autistic
and this explained most of her fears.

A mind that is intricate functioning
unique thought process working overtime,
her special way of viewing the world
was music with a different chime.

With knowing of her autism
coping skills weren't always clear,
but support from the few who understood
brought some kind of hope a little more near.

Because of her faith in God
her resilience never seemed to quit,
many of the bullies were jealous
something they would never admit.

Her power can be expressed in color
in so many amazing ways,
she really does know inside her
being different really pays.

She sometimes can tell you
that being broken isn't her only song,
and that she has inner power
and can show you she is strong.

It might take a lot of time for you all
to realize whose story was just told,
that this child learned from her brother
just how to be very bold.

There may always be certain others
who believe her spirit is dead,
but she will stand up and tell you no
I am very much alive; I am I said.

(inspired by my good friend: Mike Green)

The Empty Chair

My mom was a strong formidable women
with sparkling deep brown eyes,
and a beautiful white smile
who became accustomed to my cries.

She would be my rock
throughout my confusing life,
she was my own protector
and my father's loyal and loving wife.

First, she was my mother
and she grew to be my friend,
I knew that I was blessed
and would love her till the end.

Everyone called her Billie
papa's nickname was forever,
not many knew her real name
Billie fit her to the letter.

My mother called her parents
mama and papa from the start,
they were her strength and wisdom
she carried in her heart.

From the time I was quite little
I watched how my mom so loved her dad,
like there was no tomorrow
and this always made me feel sad.

It was like at any moment
he might be taken away,
they patted each other's backs
there was nothing more to say.

Papa suffered from a bad heart
an illness from the war,
he lived his life to the fullest
and never asked for one thing more.

Such demonstrative emotions
were a traditional family trait,
to learn to embrace family dynamics
just could never be too late.

Papa's motto to his children
was that the show always must go on,
he said this to my mother
until the day that he was gone.

My mother was a dancer
and she cut her hand before a show,
papa wrapped her hand in gauze
took her to the stage and let her go.

Strict with all expectations
growing up old school,
could sometimes seem too much
and just a little cruel.

When my mother's papa passed away
she lost a big piece of her heart,
then she lost her first-born son
and her world fell apart.

Later when my mother's mama left this earth
panic attacks hit her hard,
she was hurting all the time
which left her emotionally scarred.

Because my mother's life was often hard
she always expected a lot from me,
which caused strong effects from tough love
I had deficits she just couldn't see.

Whenever I thought something was too difficult
and couldn't handle what it might entail,
my mother urged me to get out there
and I was even more afraid to fail.

At times when I needed my mom's support
she wanted me to tough it out,
rolling with the punches
was what this attitude was all about.

When things went wrong for me
and people made me feel bad,
I needed my mom's protective love
she always knew when I was sad.

Her goal was to help me be strong
to give me tools to learn to cope,
how to focus on better days
taught me to fight for that hope.

Before boarding the bus for school
my mom would hold me tight,
I would look back at her
till she was out of sight.

We sat up alone late at night
sharing all our stories from the heart,
enjoying humor and laughing hard
I could never imagine our lives apart.

My mom was the life of every party
young people enjoyed her being around,
the room would ring with laughter
it was a wonderful sound.

My mom was all that she could be
my first home, my protector and best friend,
I needed her always in my life
and I thought this dream could never end.

As I got older and came home to visit
my mom would be seated in her favorite chair,
none of us in her family would take her spot
not one of us would even dare.

We had vast experiences throughout the years
some bad but all mostly great,
she called me her emotional sensitive daughter
her and I shared that very trait.

The day came when my mom got very ill
her prognosis was very bad,
she entirely broke everyone's heart
and death took her away from us and my dad.

The nightmares we faced were brutal
as our lives became so unfair,
etched in my mind forever more
is the sight of my mother's empty chair.

(dedicated to my Mother)

Betrayal

Do you hear me calling to you?
Why have you not answered me?
If I give up the ghost and die now
will you finally begin to see?

If you never loved me, why did you pretend?
Did you not think this would be cruel?
Isn't there some kind of ethics you must follow?
Is there not some unwritten rule?

You must realize that I gave my heart to you.
Why would you crush my every dream?
Is there some madness to your plan?
Or only a defect in your wicked scheme?

Did I only imagine that you cared?
Are all those warm thoughts only in my head?
What would you expect would happen?
That you'd come home and find me dead?

Does it make you feel happy to watch me cry?
What is your purpose in hurting me this way?
You reject all communication
it doesn't matter what I have to say.

How long do you expect to continue this abuse?
From starting when it's dark until the morning dawn.
Are you wondering what it will take
for me to at last really be gone?

Letting Go

What can I do now?
My fears have all been validated!
Does no one really care?
I know the answer to that question!

Is it true that nothing I thought was mine ever was?
I am beginning to feel my health fail!
Do I try to hold on and hope to make it better?

It will never change and it's much too late!
Will I have to go off and die alone?
I must face reality and just let go!

Timber's Whispering Wind

You find yourself gazing beyond the confines of your yard
into the distance beyond the foliage and trees,
imaging life in the woods where animals' dwell
feeling the gentle morning breeze.

You feel nature everywhere hiding
all within the protection of their own special place,
tucked away from all the intense noise
pleasantly avoiding all the chaos of the human race.

You find yourself in a calm all your own
as your mind drifts so very far away,
even as you find yourself lost
you're in a place you really want to stay.

You realize that you find such peace
in a place where noise is of a natural sound,
only the movement of the birds rustling in the trees
where only calls of nature are all around.

You can focus on much needed relaxation
a kind that only wildlife can bring,
where coyote's howl at night
and during the day the birds will sing.

Life is serene and filled with carefree running water
like a stream that ripples and carries its movement for miles,
fish live free among the waves of its endless path
helping you forget all of life's trials.

Then I think about the fast lane in human existence
living in our world where we all have sinned,
and I realize that life will not compare to nature in the woods
where the music you hear is only TIMBERS WHISPERING WIND.

(Inspired by my love of living in the woods)

The Power of the Rain

There is great power in mother nature
where her moods determine what she may bring,
she can decide to beam sunshine on the earth
or havoc with thunder and lightning may ring.

When love is in the air
her warmth may caress the earth,
She may give you the kiss of the sun
which will radiate a new kind of birth.

Or she may just be at rest with silence
with gentle drifting clouds floating by,
with the white billowy shapes
dancing across the sky.

Then when the earth becomes thirsty
and the ground becomes dry,
mother nature may develop darkness
where she may begin to cry.

Deep angry clouds may collect
and might even cause some concern,
the eye of the storm erupts
and pouring rain takes it's turn.

However, one must always remember
that mother nature does not plead,
her job is to give this earth
all that she really does need.

A bolt of lightning may come crashing down
and the sound of thunder may echo very loud,
strong winds may cause a tornado
bringing an awe-struck crowd.

People may at times need to seek shelter
and allow mother nature to release these strong winds,
there is a lesson in the eye of the storm
just as God above will forgive all our sins.

Mother nature has her own purpose
and we may not always understand,
she is one of the world's greatest mysteries
our Lord God inspires what is planned.

Some days may become dreary
with continual rain pouring from the sky,
we may become restless
and not understand the reason why.

Plants and vegetation need her nourishment
the earth has so much to gain,
only God's miracle called mother nature
understands the power of the rain.

(Inspired by my love and fascination of mother nature)

Haiku

Predetermined
People never really change
But intensely just evolve
Into their intended evil....

Cat Expression
Soft and furry silhouette
With independent souls emerge
The mystical Cat....

Blissful Spirit
Watchful eyes from darkness
Emerging from the night
Become the nocturnal Angels....

Empty Soul
Never touching the heart`
Surpasses every intimate moment
Leaving an empty vessel....

Perseverance
Trees towering above all
Bending in the wind
Eluding the ferocious storm....

Tornado
Warm and cold gasses
Twisting powerful angry wind
Leaving massive empty destruction....

Denying Choices
Patience not a virtue
Confusion controlling the mindfulness
As chances slip away....

Choose your path freely
Remembering the expected fate
Never undoing the outcome
Becomes the vast reality…

There is a price
Foolishness is mere blindness
A direction to nowhere
Reality becomes intended fate…

Follow the light
Transforming into light
Like a bursting flame
Descending into the Heavens….

Draw the positive
Showcase your every desire
Robust like limitless bliss
Inviting your chosen audience….

You got this
Marching to your destiny
Power promotes your goal
Cleansing your faithful path….

Feline Ecstasy
Zooming flash glowing eyes
Purring cozy beside me
My companion the cat….

The inevitable
Flittering by with fear
Butterfly with tattered wings
Land's itself to die….

Lost Faith
Ridicule rules tormented minds
Becoming devastation in believing
Extinguished from all hope….

Open your Soul
From the great unknown
Comes power from above
Receive his brilliant light....

Unearthly power
Unearthly powerful eternal light
Reaches your Godly soul
Granting you Heavenly rebirth....

Canine Bliss
Entity of unconditional love
Crawls inside your soul
Forever in your heart....

Dream of Love
Lose yourself in dreams
Walk away from nightmares
Make your own reality....

Destroyed by lies
Liars consume your faith
Bringing deep dark despair
You have lost yourself....

Simple is Peace
Honestly you got this
Simplicity will ease expectations
Resulting in given peace....

You are free
You see clearly now
Leaving injustice behind you
To perish in sin....

The Messenger
Bishops of His lessons
Messenger of His righteousness
God has chosen your path....

Rabid

The sting of death
Feverishly driven into madness
Seething with uncontrollable rage....

Lost Chance
Long lost memories
Like a past life
Out of your grasp....

Eagle Eyes
Eyes of the eagle
Penetrate your very existence
He will end you....

All Things Bleed
Even the grass bleeds
As it is cut
Imagine being human?

High Expectations
Basic needs of life
Surpasses your own reality
Like the impossible dream....

The Bully

Presumed to be popular
with their artificial self-worth,
living in a world of grandeur
thinking they control the earth.

With outward appearances
that they are masters of their games,
sitting on their pedestal judging others
and dishing out derogatory names.

They prey upon the fearful ones
who are different or maybe shy,
never caring about the pain they cause
or if their victims live or die.

Their extent of cruelty is relentless
as they abuse those they feel superior to,
they are in denial of all they've done
they might have felt guilty if they only knew.

With these entitled kind of people
there is no limit to their plans,
they have no idea how their victims
are at the mercy of their hands.

They taunt and tease to no end
making fun of a person is their goal,
while those who are their target
end up with a broken soul.

I've been exposed to that violence
where I've been in danger with my life,
beating caused internal damage
and cut me like a knife!

People might begin to wonder
what motivates that kind of hate,
will this trauma finally wake them up
or will it be too late?

Their kind of people are nothing special
they really are not at all great,
they all are just pathetic bullies
who might one day meet their fate.

Elderly Eyes

Feeble old man looking lost
is seated on a park bench alone,
his eyes drawn downward
wrinkles itched in his face over the years have grown.

Obviously in deep thought
scanning through his life,
he had an only child who passed away
and then later too soon he lost his wife.

Life to him isn't kind at all
only filled with memories long gone,
making him wonder in sadness
about what it is that he did wrong.

He recalls that he always worked hard
and often struggled all his life,
taking care of bills and his home
and loving his child and his wife.

He was honest and loyal
always doing just what he could,
he was decent to all those around him
and did all that every man should.

People in the park were staring at him
and could feel all his deep-seated pain,
they know with the enormous amount of hurt
this man would never be the same.

An old man who carried a heavy burden
remembering in prayer just what he said
"Oh Lord why did you leave me behind?"
wishing all the while that he was dead.

Couples in love were all he could see
young love all were passing him by,
he begged to stay with his memories
pleading to God to just let him die.

Hospital bills made him lose his home
only a shelter with strangers he shared,
as all of society continued on with their lives
he realized in confusion that nobody cared.

Loneliness and devastation became his life
his face covered in golden droplets as he cries,
his skin was streaked with redness
you could see all that he'd been through in those eyes.

The Brown Things

I remember the day long ago that hubby
came home with a surprise in a box,
two darling Australian Shepherd puppies
and boy could they talk.

They both had this cute lingo
only they could do like they did,
they would howl with a sound
just like a kid.

The howl broke out with whaaawhaaa
at the end of their bellow,
it was certainly their own way
of saying HELLO!

By the breed description they were called red
but hubby and I called them brown,
one boy was known to be feisty
the other boy was a clown.

They were litter mates so special to us
one was smaller with a smooth coat of fur,
the bigger one had a rough coat of mostly brown
we chose names that fit them for sure.

The smaller boy was feisty like a storm and hence his name
he had one solid amber eye and one solid blue,
his coat was of many shades of brown
and he was my heart dog too.

Sergeant was his bigger brother
who loved everyone he got to know,
his personality was nothing but loving
and his popularity continued to grow.

Our boys walked in the woods
always at my side,
they were my heartbeat
and often my guide.

We played many fun games
over the years we shared,
they were the best friends
I knew always cared.

Both of the boys played flyball
and were admired by every crowd,
they were awesome at the game
and made us so very proud.

Storm was reactive in the line ups
and got into trouble at times,
but we always defended him
with all of his crimes.

Sergeant ran the course
so obediently for many a friend,
he was special to a lot of people
he started his own trend.

The boys were lovingly called
our little brown things,
a phrase we remember
for the laughter it brings.

It was hard to be too serious
with such fun-loving dogs,
they loved playing games
jumping like frogs.

Sergeant and Storm filled our lives
with nothing but joy and fun,
they were both legends
and were second to none.

Those brown things had beauty
charisma, loyalty, and charm,
we always felt safe with them
they kept us from harm.

When the day came
that Sergeant fell ill,
we shuddered at the thought
and the earth stood still.

We laid with our Sergeant
pouring out all our tears,
Sergeant licked them away
loving us more than his fears.

Dogs love you more than themselves
always bravely comforting you with their love,
instead of worrying about their own pain
they endlessly hold you above.

Sergeant passed away at home
and took our hearts far away,
a tumor erupted on his spine
it was a terribly sad day.

It wasn't all so long
that storm followed his brother,
but we knew they would be together
and they so loved each other.

Hubby and I mourn our great loss
each and every day,
we wish that life
wasn't this way.

One day we both know
when our time comes to leave this earth,
that Sergeant and Storm will be waiting
with the glory of rebirth.

Give it your All

The trees in the woods are dancing
the wind is tickling their inner core,
flowers are starting to break ground
summer is about to bring a whole lot more.

The air is smelling fresh and clean
old man winter is washed away by rain,
the rabbits are running across the ground
while squirrels in the trees are raising cane.

Berries are filling up the bushes
vegetation is growing everywhere,
there is plenty of nourishment for wildlife
and especially for the deer and bear.

Nature cries are booming happily
the birds are mating and singing their song,
and soon the woods will be so alive
all new birth will come along.

Humankind will emerge from their homes
working on projects in the great outdoors,
accomplishing important tasks
that were left over from the season before.

Children will leave their computers indoors
and the internet will have much less tweets,
replaced by robust play and the sound of laughter
as the little people fill the streets.

Neighbors will be cooking out
while the smell of burgers will fill the air,
everyone will gather with their friends
bringing a dish or drink to share.

Heat will bring people to the beach
enjoying the warm weather in the sun,
volleyball and games will be played
with lots of laughter and fun.

Hanging out with picnic baskets
while dogs are playing in the park,
you will hear people are chattering
while all the playful dogs will bark.

When the day comes to an end
and the sunset brings out a full moon,
people will party the night away
and often will sleep until noon.

Always value all that you've got
take time to enjoy what God has made,
create memories that will stay with you
and cherish always how you played.

All living things come to an end,
so never allow yourself to live in fear,
give it your all as long as you can
and the earth will know that you were here.

Be the Storm

Heat rises, and the wind stands still
puffy clouds turn dark and dense,
turbulence erupts from the sky
and seeking shelter is our only defense.

Off in the distance is a rumbling sound
until it becomes threatening and bold,
beware of the electricity in the air
is what we've all been told.

Crackling from dark cloud to the earth
comes a rod of lightning followed by a thud,
the pouring rain breaks loose
and the ground is soaked with a lot of mud.

Shimmering in the night is the storm
sounding frantic and loud,
a nervous twister is spotted
drawing an awe-struck crowd.

As the blackness turns vile
as the wind picks up speed,
swirling in a circle of rage
frightened hearts began to plead.

Down to the cellar we all run
now hovering on the floor,
as siding is ripped from the home
and there goes the door.

Demolished like paper
flattened to the ground,
is many a home in the area
as the warning siren begins to sound.

Then from out of nowhere
comes a silence at last,
we emerge from the basement
because the threatening storm has passed.

Looking at the wreckage left behind
filled with panic we hop in a car,
remembering the devastation
speeding away to somewhere quite far.

In spite of the anger of the storm
we pick up the pieces left behind,
the community comes together
to show that they are kind.

We are the most invincible humans
who build our homes back,
we all work in harmony
and get our lives back on track.

A storm may come and go
but is no match for courage and pride,
we brave each storm that comes
because just like us, the earth has cried.

Have respect for the storm
but don't allow it to consume all you are,
you know you've bravely survived
and outlived them thus far.

A storm is truly a part of life
it will come again one night,
have faith in God
and do what is right.

Life isn't promised to be easy
so, you must fight back,
in times when things get tough
plan your attack.

Remember, you are the storm
throughout your time on this earth,
you were destined for greatness
from the time of your birth.

What Kind of People are We?

What kind of people are we?
Does the P stand for Positive?
Does the E stand for Entertaining?
Does the O stand for Optimistic?
Does the second P stand for Personable?
Does the L stand for Loving?
Does the second E stand for Extraordinary?
Or are we the other kind of people?
Where the P stands for Persecuting.
Where the E stands for Envy.
Where the O stands for Obstinate.
Where the second P stands for Pessimistic.
Where the L stands for Loss.
and where the second E stands for End?
What kind of people are we?

Can we be supportive and caring
and someone's shoulder to cry on,
or are we only going to be selfish
and just always be gone?

Can we be helpful and tender
to make others feel safe and sound,
or will we be shallow and distant
and just not be around?

Can we be accepting and sharing
so, others know that we care,
or will we be indifferent and vain
and be completely unaware?

Can we live in God's image
so that we all win,
or will we be nothing but evil
and wallow in sin?

What choices we make
about whom we want to be,
will be dependent upon our ethic's
for the entire world to see.

So, what kind of people are we
the one's who do what is decent and good,
or the ones who know better
but never do what we should?

Make your decision right now
let the whole world see,
that we are God's children
that is what kind of people are we.

You Must Learn to Dance in the Rain

Find joy in the small things
take it all in,
never wait for just the right time
to let it begin.

Don't wait for a special occasion
to make that trip for ice cream,
joy is not scheduled
but comes like a dream.

Don't plan for that perfect weather
have that party right now,
live in the moment always
as much as life will allow.

Wear that new outfit
no one is promised tomorrow,
you must take the good with the bad
the joy and the sorrow.

If you love to sing
you don't have to be a rock star,
it's the feeling it gives you
not the guitar.

Shout from the mountain tops
and celebrate each day like it's your last,
your life is not a perfect story
you don't need a professional cast.

Laugh and act silly
and don't worry what others will think,
be random and creative
and give us all a wink.

If you love certain foods
that you know you shouldn't eat,
go for it anyway
and call it a treat.

Happiness isn't planned
the way we often believe that it should be,
let the chips fall where they may
and set yourself free.

Run bare foot on the beach
let the sand sift through your toes,
feel the comfort of nature.
it's the small pleasures that glow.

Don't worry about gossip
or who is with who,
fretting the small stuff
will make you feel blue.

Take that big chance
as often as you can,
don't focus on details
you don't need a plan.

Go skinny dipping by moonlight
and let yourself loose,
take a taste of something different
drink a variety of that juice.

If things don't seem to be in your favor
try something new,
there will be someone out there
you never know who.

Life is about experiences
a box of chocolates to choose,
that might bring something better
so, you really can't lose.

Wake up with excitement in your heart
you never know what a new day may bring,
love could be right around the corner
you might get that ring.

When you're met with disappointment
remember opportunities come along every day,
if something doesn't work out
at least you can play.

Try if you will – to face fears you have,
don't let them take that control,
beating all the odds
must be your ultimate goal.

You may have heard this before
and it might sound the same,
but you must always be willing
to dance in the rain.

Work in Progress

Where we live is our palace
our place to retreat,
the spot where we go to rest
when we are beat.

Our shelter is our home
where we can relax and find peace,
we can hop in our beds
buried in blankets of fleece.

We sit with our families
having dinner each night,
where we are free to be in harmony
or we can even argue and fight.

Many secrets are held
behind those confined walls,
where we can do our own thing
until duty calls.

We can lounge on our coach
dreaming all day,
enjoying our fantasies
then can go out and play.

We spend time just doing nothing
or sometimes working nonstop,
we can sit and watch a movie
and have treats and a pop.

Our home is our haven
where we decide what we want to do,
we make many decisions
or maybe plans to do something new.

We put time and energy
into improvements we need,
we might help with projects
or we might just lead.

Painting and rearranging
new furniture or decor,
we can remodel a room
and do even more.

Our safe place is ours
to do what we will,
we can spend the day cleaning
or go outside to grill.

We can personalize our walls
with family photos and a clock,
we might want to build something special
or just sit there and talk.

At the end of each day
we know improvements were made,
we secure our kingdom
and keep those bills paid.

We take pride in our home
and often invite over a friend,
we feel proud for our efforts
until the days end.

Whether our special place is just square
or shaped like a dome,
it is our sanctuary
a place we call home.

Just a Little Sick Humor

You try to sleep in
but find yourself wide awake
you hop out of bed
and feel like your bones might break.

You step down on the carpet
into some soft slimy cat puke,
your feet slip out from under you
a disastrous fluke.

As you come crashing down on your back
you feel yourself slide across the floor,
and smell the puke on the back of your head
right about now, you wish you were dead.

Limping to the bathroom
to wash it out of your hair,
your husband comes down the hall
and gives you a stare.

Breakfast is served by the hubby
the bread is a crispy critter,
the water you drink
all tastes quite bitter.

You realize your day
has only just begun,
if it continues like this
you might look for a gun.

You intend to take a nice shower
but the wash has taken all the hot water,
you try to imagine that it is
just a little bit hotter.

You jump out of the shower
soap still in your hair,
what happens next
just isn't fair.

Another slip and fall
right onto the floor,
you come crashing forward
and are hit by the door.

You are shivering and shaking
not sure what to do next,
you look up to the sky
and think you are hexed.

Just a little time resting on the bed
to try to calm down,
so that later in the day
you can go into town.

You wonder out loud
why all the bad luck,
you just got out of bed
and feel like you were hit by a truck.

The dogs are barking
and begging to go out,
your head is hurting
so, you began to shout.

Then you discover the dogs
have crapped on the floor,
you just don't know
if you can take much more.

You and your hubby head into town
to get some food,
waiting in a long line
and the cashier is nothing but rude.

You think to yourself
she didn't have a morning like mine,
maybe she should smoke some pot
and have herself a few glasses of wine.

You have ice cream melting
and end up in a traffic jam,
the entire carton gets runny
and sinks into your ham.

You hope to get moving quickly
to get back home as fast as you can manage
then someone has a three-car accident
and you get involved in the damage.

Now waiting for a tow truck
with all melted food,
you know your next meal
will obviously be crude.

You actually are pretty banged up,
you realize this when the police arrive,
you have a pounding headache
and your car won't drive.

There you both are
in a hospital waiting room,
as long as they took
you might meet your doom.

Then you are shocked to notice
that you have cuts all over your face,
maybe they can take you to the psych ward
instead of that place.

It takes the entire day to be discharged
and you're all covered with stitches and gauze,
you want to put your day on fast speed rewind
and then if you're lucky you can hit the pause.

You get home at last with no vehicle
so, your hubby decides to cook you a meal,
his kind gesture for you
is really a big deal.

You rest in your room until you see smoke
you rush to the kitchen to inquire,
then to your disbelief
your house is on fire.

Your meal is burnt again
but is not your biggest worry,
the Fire Truck comes
in a hell of a hurry.

They hose your house down
and even inside,
no wonder you're nuts
and lost it and cried.

The fire department might sue
and water damaged all your stuff,
as if the rest of your day
just wasn't enough!

Don't worry too much though
day has come to an end,
you're hoping the bad luck is over
but tomorrow you can do it all again.

Chocolate

My favorite of all candy
a sweet and delicious taste,
it can heal any ill
it's never a waste.

It melts in your mouth
with its rich eye watering flavor,
the pleasure you feel eating it
can be your savior.

You name one thing
that chocolate can't do,
most people are lovers
no matter who.

You can eat chocolate in a bar
or on top of ice cream,
it tickles your tummy
you might have to scream.

Bring me some chocolate
and bring it right now,
I will eat it as much
as time will allow.

I'm old enough to eat it
and not get any zits,
living without chocolate
would really be the pits.

It's brown thick texture
brings out a smile,
I need that chocolate fix
at least for a while.

Chocolate is second to none,
it is simply the best treat,
a day without it
just isn't complete.

Whether it's melted and hot
running down your chin,
or thick, crisp and luscious
you'll be the happiest you've ever been.

It will stain your cloths
if left there to dry,
not being able to have it
will make you cry.

You will lick your fingers
and even your face,
till nothing is left
not even a trace.

I want some chocolate
because it is the best,
any candy expert
can be put to the test.

If it's not all that
as we've claimed it will be,
you just taste that chocolate
and you will agree.

Deep in Thought

As I sit staring up at the cloudy sky
I remember times gone by,
the sadness I feel deep inside
makes me feel I might die.

The loneliness is overwhelming
and crippling in a certain way,
I pray that those responsible
one day will pay.

I watch those cruel people
hurt others and just never see,
how their lives remain the same
but what about me?

They make sure that I'm shut out
and black balled from all that I do,
it really crushes my spirit
if they only knew.

Those hateful type of people
will create situations that are not fair,
only concerned about their lives
and just never will care.

Watching things, I can no longer do
I sit on the outside looking in,
turning a life upside down
is really a sin.

I long for the fun I once knew
and the desires I had,
I know that I'm a caring person
and never was bad.

People often misunderstand me
and just look the other way,
they don't care at all
what I have to say.

I wonder if I was like them
and how that would feel,
but know that it's not possible
and not one single bit real.

I've come to the conclusion
that I can only be me,
where is that acceptance
why can't they see?

Sitting alone with reflection
of all those days gone by,
I am not at fault
because I really did try.

Be like the others
my mom use to say,
because I am so unique
they won't let me play.

As I sit here alone
so deep in thought,
my crime is being different
is all I was taught,

I guess I will always
have to accept being alone,
and stay away from people
if I'd only known.

We all wish for someone
maybe one special friend,
that may never happen
so, it might be the end.

I can only remember
that I always tried,
maybe they will understand me
once I have died.

Unseasonably Cold

As it nears the end of the month
May will soon bring in June,
we are behind in the season
and barely in bloom.

By this time last year
flowers were everywhere,
it doesn't seem like summer
it just won't even compare.

The leaves are barely seen
on all of the trees,
the weather is too cold
the greater percentage agrees.

I pity the warm weather birds
that thrive in the summer heat,
the ground is still cold
under their feet.

Many of the bushes are stunted
and not growing as they should,
wishing we could change the temperature
if we only could.

The rains are so constant
we need the sun bad,
all summer critters
look very sad.

Summer doesn't last long enough,
in even the usual season,
we've exhausted all thoughts
and don't know the reason.

Strong high-powered wind
is taking trees down,
as they are splitting and breaking
with a devastating sound.

Will we even have summer
this season at all?
Will any of the trees and vegetation
grow up proud and tall?

Usually by now the temperatures
are toasty and warm,
this cold weather
is bringing us harm.

We are missing so much
the best part of our lives,
baby birds should be chirping
and many beehives.

Nature needs to continue
to progress in a natural way,
without this change
it holds wildlife at bay.

Please bring us warm weather
and beautiful sunshine,
so, we can enjoy grilling
and being outside to dine.

Summers are important
as is natures game,
without our warm weather
it just isn't the same.

This chill in the air
is getting really old,
too much disappointment
with it unseasonably cold.

Real True Love

Remember the three kinds of love
"IF, BECAUSE OF, and IN SPITE OF,"
the "IF" is conditional and fake
the "BECAUSE OF" is also not real love.

If you think you love someone
if they do this thing or that,
the relationship is doomed
that's not where it's at.

If you think you love a person
"BECAUSE OF" just what you need,
you are expecting certain things
and will never succeed.

Loving someone in "SPITE OF" it all
shows your honesty and integrity,
you cherish the good and bad,
you accept all that you see.

If a person is good looking
and can jump start your heart,
when they lose their looks
you will end up apart.

You will need something lasting
and that is their beauty inside,
expecting them to have good looks
is nothing but your own selfish pride.

Accept a person's short comings
as much as their good side,
if you can do this
you know you have tried.

If that person makes a mistake
and your love remains stable,
you can build them up
as much as you're able.

Working together always
makes your relationship strong,
with this kind of power
you can never go wrong.

It's much more important
to face adversity as a whole,
this gives you ammunition
adds character to your soul.

At times a person you love
may fall behind,
hold them up
and do what is kind.

To help your partner
give them your time,
to accept a person's weakness
is never a crime.

None of us are perfect
we all have a flaw,
always be supportive
like an unwritten law.

So, learn all about
how to put your partner above,
no matter what happens
this is the only true love.

Flowers Come Back

The ground erupts
emerges a tiny stem of green,
the sun nourishes the life
as in natures scheme.

Ever so slowly
the plants will grow,
as time carefully lapses
all the beauty will show.

As tiny buds open up
a sweet smell in the air,
such a pleasant fragrance
they bloom in God's care.

Colors of the rainbow
all in a neat line,
they will fill up the garden
in their own sweet time.

Rain comes down from the heavens
in its own plentiful way,
the beautiful flowers
we wish would all stay.

Summer is filled with precious life
up until the warmth will end,
as the seasons change
the cold weather will soon begin.

The once beautiful flowers go dormant
and shrivel to the ground,
as old man winter takes over
empty gardens are all around.

Remember summer will be back
there is no reason to fret,
it is part of God's plan
to have no regret.

The different seasons take turns
to govern the earth,
our flowers bring back their fragrance
and have their rebirth.

Broken

My life started out
with an older brother,
he was my hero
like no other.

Just as I became school age
my big brother passed away,
with this amount of pain
there is nothing more to say.

Childhood illness took him from us
making me the oldest,
he went to live with God
is what my parents told us.

My world became lonely
like an empty void,
I felt confused
life was destroyed.

Dealing with a disability
that was hidden for years,
a neurological disorder
that nothing cures.

I didn't realize
why I felt so alone,
I knew I was quite different
and this I could own.

I struggled with life
as the years passed by,
when people didn't accept me
alone I would cry.

My peers in school
made fun of me,
even the teachers
would have to agree.

I looked for friendship
whenever I could,
some were short lived
and that wasn't good.

At times I had a best friend
or at least I thought that I did,
when they betrayed me
I ran off and hid.

I took things hard
it hurt me so bad,
but it's hard to miss
what I never had.

My family dynamic's
weren't my best support,
I sometimes felt abandon
I have to report.

I lived in a world
where I was often confused,
people would bully me
I always felt used.

Learning was difficult
in the style I was taught,
every day was a challenge
for acceptance I fought.

When people misunderstood
all I would do,
the deficit became overwhelming
the damage just grew.

I faced dysfunction
in so many ways,
I would be in turmoil
during all those days.

So I guess I will say
I am what I live,
still my heart was golden
with all I would give.

Certain good people
who were caring souls,
helped me succeed
and accomplish some goals.

The very few people
who saw me inside,
gave me the strength
and they knew how I tried.

The cruel rejections
were around my neck like a token,
it is really no wonder
I ended up broken.

Only My Way

A wild child
with eyes like the skies,
sensitive and caring
who lives in goodbyes.

A child confused
with a look of doubt,
always so hyper
running about.

With parents who complained
she was a little bit strange,
she did things her way
so far out of range.

Her mother worked hard
to have her conform,
but she was always so different
like an unpredictable storm.

Her mother wanted her
to just be able to fit in,
but she had to be herself
and they just couldn't win.

Her head was so busy
always up in a cloud,
it seemed impossible
to make her mom proud.

A different operating system
misunderstood by others,
the subject of ridicule
from the other mothers.

She always stood out
just like a sore thumb,
unusually creative
and never was dumb.

She was so off the wall
incredibly odd and unique,
curious to see her in action
other parents wanted to hear her speak.

Often her own parents
were embarrassed by her,
they never knew what next
was about to occur.

The child was so impulsive
collecting bugs in the garden,
neighbors would not
give her a pardon.

She also would catch
turtles and a snake,
but nothing about her
was ever fake.

She laid out her faults
like jewels on a table,
never hiding her difference
nor was she able.

So often a face
covered with dirt,
she had so much fun
how could it hurt?

Her parents were devastated
and appalled by her behavior,
they prayed to God
that He could save her.

Mom and dad only wanted
her to be like all of her peers,
they tried to hush her
there were too many ears.

This child would say
unconventional things,
only her parents knew
the gossip it brings.

It was always a battle
and a task to behold,
other parents would shun her
and they would act really cold.

Her journey was a series
of outrageous events,
her parents often would scold her
with their angry vents.

This unusual poor child
would be forced to sit down,
and endure their anger
wearing that terrifying frown.

When a child is autistic
this frustration won't work,
just an example
of one more quirk.

In spite of her trauma
with things her parents would say,
this unconventional child
did it her way.

(Inspired by the song: I DID IT MY WAY FROM the perspective of an
AUTISTIC CHILD.)

My Man

You meet the one
when you least expect,
and later in your life
you look back and reflect.

I met the love of my life
at a friend's wedding,
we were both surprised
by the way we were heading.

He was a little clean cut
but a good-looking man,
I got him to grow a beard
and get a nice tan.

I opened up the wild in him
and although he was sensitive,
he could show the rugged side
and that's the way we lived.

He was my friend's uncle
was the uncanny part of it all,
I was more than grateful
and he was a little off the wall.

My man was talented
and good at most things he tried,
our lives became an adventure
we shared laughter and pride.

The most important part of him
is that his heart was always good,
he really aimed to please
and did what he could.

A man who loved animals
and was kind to an extreme,
the wonderful things he accomplished
was more than a dream.

Dogs and cats were our family
we rescued and cared for many,
the love we had for them
was wholesome and plenty.

My man cared for them when they were sick
always stayed by their side,
he would hold them for hours
even when they died.

My man is filled with light inside
and it glows day and night,
the closeness we share
grew overnight.

When I feel alone and sad
my man holds me tight,
his gentle caring soul
shows me we'll be alright.

Most importantly I have to say
is that my man is true,
he was sent by God above
I think I always knew.

Our love has braved the test of time
and has become far more than strong,
together we face all the storms
even surviving when things go wrong.

I love my man so very much
that all I need to be,
is in his loving arms
those who know us must agree.

I remember my father telling me
I can see the love you share,
he is a lot like my dad
no one can compare.

I am hoping that one day
when we cease to exist,
that I die in my man's arms
with his gentle kiss.

(Inspired by my LOVE for my hubby 🖤)

Wood Ticks, Mosquitos and Gnats

Summer is filled with blood sucking bugs
Wood Ticks, Mosquito's, and Gnat's,
spreading illness to everyone
they're as bad as little bats!

They spread disease to living things
many with fatal results,
they swarm in hoards in the air
just like those little cults!

They spoil summer days
with their relentless bite,
the way they consume the earth
is a constant continual fight.

People go inside at night
covered in many a painful welt,
they itch and burn and hurt
a feeling I know we all have felt.

The Wood Tick is an ugly grey bug
whose bellies will fill with blood,
a Mosquito stings with their long needle
and fill the air like a flood.

Gnat's love to fly in your eyes
they take big chunks out of your skin,
battling with blood sucking bugs
is how it's always been.

We use bug sprays with their toxic smells
and will fog the air when we think we should,
it's not safe around food or drink
and it never does any good.

We detest that buzzing sound
the Mosquito and the Gnat makes,
and the gross swelling they leave behind
then the Wood Tick fills up and breaks.

We end up with ugly red itchy bumps
blood suckers are nasty and vile,
they put a damper on all the fun
and wipe away your smile.

Chem trails are often used
as a desperate and last resort,
those toxins cause cancer
science has to report.

Wood Ticks, Mosquito's, and Gnat's
they die off when old man winter wakes,
it has to get cold before they will leave
it's sad to know what it takes.

Wicked Twister

Grey skies all day
deadly skies at night,
something looked off
and just wasn't right.

Gradually as evening fell
the weather turned worse,
the skies became black and threatening
like it was about to burst.

The rains came like a monsoon
and flowed down like a waterfall,
huge trees were flying in the air
they were fifty some feet tall.

Strong winds ripped through the woods
as the rage of the storm turned to ramped swirls,
along with the large hail
that looked like golf ball sized perils.

The fence in the back of the house
was flattened to the ground,
the frantic pressure of trees falling
made a loud thumping sound.

Thunder boomed and shook the ground
followed by the blaze of lightning,
as its power scorched the earth
and became a little more frightening.

The cats ran about the house
looking for a place to hide,
if any of us had been outside
I think we would have surely died.

Glowing eyes in the dark
with that scared puzzled look,
thunder continued on all night
as all the windows shook.

In the path of destruction
was a growling atmosphere,
by the way it looked outside
we all thought the end was near.

Suddenly the ferocious electric storm
made the lights go out,
everyone inside their homes
were running all about.

Gathering flashlights
candles with many other sources,
families were hindered
by nature's outstanding forces.

No running water to use
all comforts completely gone,
still no power back on
during the next days early dawn.

There were puddles in the yard
trees across the fence,
even in the driveway
this disaster made us all tense.

It actually took most of the day
for the power to come back on,
but the threat of more to come
really isn't gone.

Wicked twister stay away
we can't handle anymore,
but the skies are still dark right now
just like before.

(Inspired by the past day's events)

Don't Mess With Me

I must warn the world
never mess with me,
you will not like the results
of what you just might see.

I stay in my own business
and worry about me and mine,
everything I work to do
is good and turns out fine.

I am very articulate
a person with high morals,
for you to invade my privacy
will bring you major quarrels.

I've been bullied endlessly
and will protect my life,
if you want trouble
it will cause you only strife.

Don't underestimate me
and who I am inside,
you try to destroy my reputation
all will know you have lied.

I am not your punching bag
nor someone who complied,
so, if you plan to hurt me
you will regret you even tried.

Keep your accusations to yourself
they fall upon deaf ears,
I've proven my accomplishments
over many years.

I do what I know is right
and always keep it real,
you will shortly find out
how I really feel.

I am a kind person
who wants to help a friend,
but if you betray my trust
your time with me will end.

You may believe you're superior
that you are above the law,
but your vindictive intentions
is all that others ever saw.

If you insist upon hurting me
I will reveal your evil plan,
it's best to abort your mission
if there is a chance that you can.

Putting someone else down
might be your only choice,
because you can't measure up
and have truly lost your voice.

Good people will not listen
to someone who is mean,
who spends their entire life
devoted to an evil scheme.

If you want the world to listen
you must remember who you are,
trying to ruin another person's life
will never get you very far.

I have a lot of fight in me
that you just might not see,
working to destroy me
will never set you free.

If you think your hatefulness
will ever keep me down,
It will only make me stronger
is what I have always found.

When you work to condemn me
you only reveal your biggest flaw,
by defaming my character
you're only breaking the law.

I focus on what I have to do
and work to make things right,
I don't have to prove myself to you
I'm convinced you're not too bright.

I believe we're all equal
until we prove we're not,
working on my own success
is a belief that I was taught.

My honest advice to all of you
and I think we will agree,
is that I am telling everyone
don't mess with me.

Is it All Really Worth it?

Is it all really worth it
or isn't the world all that,
are things even interesting
or are they old hat?

Do you want to be involved
or just keep to yourself,
is it worth the hassle
or bad for your health?

Do you find friendship
as something that you need,
or are most people selfish
and filled with only greed?

Has your life been successful
or just a disappointment all the way,
do you want to interact
or have nothing more to say?

Have you been accepted
for just who you are,
or have you been a reject
in your life so far?

Do you have any intentions
to try to make your life fun,
or does your gut feeling
tell you to get up and run?

Do you think there is a better plan
that might get you more results,
or are you pretty sure
it will reveal all your faults?

Where do you expect to be
in the next decade,
will it be worth your while
or will you just get played?

Is there any future for you
that will bring you happiness,
or will you only remember
the things you will miss?

Are there ever improvements
in how you see yourself,
or will you be left behind
while others have all the wealth?

Will you one day be all alone
without your spouse at your side,
or will your experience here on earth
be a pleasant ride?

Will bad fortune follow you
and you will never fit,
leaving you wondering
is it all really worth it?

Neurologically Typical Verses Autistic

NT stands for Neurologically Typical
and the term autistic is what it is,
there is much to learn
so, try to take the quiz.

If you only see what is obvious
and never see what is inside,
if you judge a book by its cover
then you have never even tried.

There is so much more to a person
than what they might appear to be,
if you learn to take the time to care
you'll be very surprised at what you see.

If you are neurologically typical
you base opinions on only what you know,
if you refuse to explore the autistic world
there's a chance your mind will never grow.

Autistic folks want awareness
so, they can share with everyone,
they wish to bridge the gap
open mindedness is how to get that done.

Acceptance is the only route
to make that connection real,
the road to that kind of success
depends on how you learn to deal.

The NT world needs to know
autism isn't negative or bad,
bringing us all together
is what we wish we had.

It will take some hard work
for us to all see eye to eye,
if it never happens for us
then I guess we'll have to say goodbye.

Autistic people were born this way
and they are who they are,
many of us have been rejected
in our confusing life thus far.

Autism isn't curable
and people dwell on a silly quirk,
for those who are judgmental
this just will never work.

We have things about our minds
that just cannot be changed,
it is our make-up from our birth
and can never be rearranged.

NT people view the world
based on what the majority will say,
while autistic people see it all
in their own special way

NT'S are influenced by society
and what is considered as the norm,
while the autistic values in this life
come in a very different form.

NT's see what only meets the eye
and will think inside the box,
Autistic people are intricate
and don't understand how the world talks.

An NT is a person who does conform
like white picket fences all in a row,
and autistic people are not sure
if they are a friend or foe.

To be neurologically typical
they must always be clear,
because they have to comply
and run from what they fear.

Autism sees things in a different light
not always cut and dry,
they function based on their experience
like the shapes of clouds passing by.

Although the autism community
may just not fit your perfect style,
you may learn to accept them
if you're open minded for a while.

Everything could be much better
if people were loved for who they are,
and each of us could fill that sky
like another twinkling star.

My Daddy

Dee Da Deet Deet dee
Da Deet Deet dee,
the little blue-eyed girl
daddy bounced me on his knee.

It's funny how I remember
the silly things we use to do,
daddy sang those goofy songs to me
and that was all I knew.

I didn't realize what it meant
but it tickled me inside,
he often made me laugh
and teased when I cried.

My daddy was a prankster
he enjoyed being funny,
I was just his baby girl
his little precious honey.

Daddy called me little Lu Lu
a tom boy in the comic strips,
ever since I was little
we went on these fishing trips.

My daddy was my hero
he gave that little push,
I would jump out and scare him
from hiding in the bush.

Of course, daddy was not afraid
and only pretended to be scared,
we had fun playing silly games
so many memories we shared.

Daddy was a fisherman
who loved the great outdoors,
he loved to filet our fish
and do all those chores.

Daddy could make caramel corn
in this big gigantic pot,
he also made the best stew
better than we ever bought.

My daddy made me feel safe
whenever I was scared,
and I always felt secure
no one else could compare.

When I did something wrong
and mom told him I was bad,
he would get really scary
but he knew I would be sad.

My daddy had such big hands
everyone commented that he did,
when he was angry at us
I ran off and hid.

Daddy liked to repeat things
and often it made me mad,
it was another way of teasing
but he was still my dad.

As I got a little older
we didn't always see eye to eye,
I became frustrated with him
and never knew the reason why.

Then when daddy got really old
I realized how much he loved me,
even though we had our fights
and didn't always agree.

Daddy was important to me
and when he passed away,
I wrote him a nice poem
and had so much to say.

I read it at his funeral
and it came from the heart,
I never thought the day would come
that we would have to part.

I will never forget him
and miss him every single day,
his tough love made me strong
it was just his way.

Daddy, I will always love you
and remember all we did,
I wish I could relive the past
and could always be a kid.

True Friends

Anything worth having
takes more effort than you know,
both parties must work hard
for friendship to ever grow.

If something seems one sided
and only one of you will give,
it doesn't matter if you're rich or poor
nor does it matter where you live.

Friendship should be equal
you need to give as much as you take,
a relationship is built on trust
otherwise, you're nothing but a fake.

Be sure you always listen
to what others have to say,
a friend can't always have the floor
it doesn't work that way.

You must always show interest
not only expect to be heard,
or another friend won't care
or listen to a word.

Both parties are important
each of you should matter,
otherwise, that friendship
will break down and shatter.

If a friend hurts your feelings
they must be willing to take the blame,
because if they think they're always right
nothing will ever be the same.

If you're wrong and you know it
be willing to apologize,
the reward goes to the friend
who truly really tries.

People will lose interest
with a door that swings one way,
that friend must always value you
if they want you to stay.

When your friend really needs you
you must be there to hear them out,
or the relationship becomes weak
and is only filled with doubt.

You must be worthy of their time
things can't only be your way,
if you insist upon being selfish
you will have to pay.

No one is going to trust you
if they're just a second thought,
to know how to be sharing
is something we were taught.

Equality in a relationship
is a strong message till the end,
then you will be considered
a real and true friend.

Eat a Treat

In the beginning of your day
you think about some food,
you eat what makes you happy
depending on your mood.

Come and join me in the dining room
you can take a seat,
I will make you something tasty
with some delicious meat.

Maybe I'll fry up some sausage patty's
dripping with their juicy flavor,
with scrambled eggs on the side
let me be your savior.

I will drink my ice water
and you can have your coffee,
for dessert we can have ice cream
with a squirt of chocolate toffy.

Lunch can be a juicy burger
with bacon and some cheese,
we can throw on some french fries
or anything you please.

Then for supper we can go out
to have lobster and your leafy salad,
I'll have some jumbo shrimp
we can make this date valid.

Then later in the evening
we can have big bowls of popcorn,
I guess we were made to splurge
that's the reason we were born.

Food is so wonderful and satisfying
so very mouthwatering and good,
we dream of eating all day long
if we only could.

Garlic cheese bread and lasagna
spaghetti or french toast,
we can fill our bellies
and be the world's greatest host.

You can create a pasta with any meat
and make a surprise meal,
there is so many variables
according to how you feel.

Being hungry is a pleasure
when you sit down to pork,
like tacos or burritos
where you don't need a fork.

Don't forget to have some desert
ice cream, cake, or pie,
cover it with whipped cream
now don't you be shy.

Because tomorrow is uncertain
eat all you can right now,
don't you worry what people say
or if they call you a sow.

At least the world will always know
that you enjoyed to eat,
don't worry what they think of you
just have another treat.

Our Fur Kids Come First

Life can be overwhelming
with too much demanding work,
but our dogs and cats are worth it
they are our one and only perk.

Hubby and I truly care the very most
about critters such as a dog or cat,
they make our lives much more enjoyable
to us that is always where it's at.

When they're not feeling well
we often sit up all night,
we stay by their side
until we know things will be alright.

A dog or cat to us is happiness
of a special fulfilling kind,
of all the successful things we do
that's when we've really shined.

We saved many dogs and cats
from situations that were bad,
who were abandon or abused,
and this made us very sad.

We spend our time saving and caring for animals
which brings out the best in both of us,
there is nothing more rewarding
than earning all their trust.

We have taken on some hard cases
where these animals were terribly scared,
we changed their nervous dispositions
because of how much we've always cared.

Many times the ones we save
show us how grateful they really are,
without our love and dedication
they would not have come this far.

We have the awesome reputation
of an animal savoir and lover,
many folks bring them to us
when our success they do discover.

Our goodness follows us everywhere
and we are happy we can give,
there is nothing we love more than knowing
all the animals that will live.

Dogs defend you with their lives
and always take you first,
they will not ever forget
how you took away their thirst.

You give them the best food to eat
and nourish their happy soul,
they look forward to fresh water
and the delicious treat they find in their bowl.

Cats you save show their gratitude
and it always is displayed,
with the way they stay so close to you
your kindness will be repaid.

The purring soothes your heart with peace
and you always know your needed,
both a dog and cat show you how they feel
with the special way you're always greeted.

If you're low on cash during the month
your animals will come first,
their enrichment in your lives
makes your heart almost burst.

You have done your best to help
and you do it all willingly,
your animals are safe with you
and God will set them free.

Our Beautiful Property

Because of owning other homes
hubby and I finally got this place,
we have never had one like this
where we can live at our own pace.

The others were special
in their own way,
but this place is awesome
I think we're going to stay.

We lived near my folks
and started out in town,
being so close to many people
always got us down.

We love to live in peace
and needed all this space,
we didn't like being hemmed in
with people in our face.

We love our country life
and if we want friends around,
we can invite them here
and then they can go back to town.

The second place we had
was actually out of state,
there were a lot of problems
we moved before it was too late.

Then coming back to Minnesota
we felt relieved to be back home,
this place was like a cabin
shaped a lot like a dome.

It was filled with knotty pine
with vaulted ceilings everywhere,
but the land was not enough
a lack of space living there.

Moving way up north
was always my biggest dream,
this place we found at last
is my fantasy and wildest scheme.

We worked hard to fix it up
some things needed care,
but soon we discovered
not another could compare.

We live on over forty acres
in the middle of the woods,
because it was less money
we bought many new goods.

We got rooms of furniture
and had nice windows installed,
we paid a small fortune
to have all our belongings hauled.

We were literally overwhelmed
and the move nearly did us in,
but this is our forever home
the best place we've ever been.

We trim our lawns around the home
with strategy and pride,
but to get to this point
was one hell of a ride.

We have an American flag
erected in the front of the yard,
we keep everything tidy
always working very hard.

I planted a long row of bushes
that travel up the hill,
watching them growing madly
really gives me a thrill.

Lilac's being my most favorite
such a variety of every kind,
eventually they'll be a big hedge
I am thrilled they are mine.

There are no neighbors
for miles all around,
no noise to have to tolerate
the only noise is a nature sound.

Our four-bedroom home
is unique and spacious,
we are still in awe
and feel so very gracious.

We use one bedroom
as our own cozy place,
two of them are hobby rooms
the last is a guest space.

A family room on the lower level
right next to our dog rooms,
that is a place where they sleep
and where we do their grooms.

Our living room upstairs is nice
where we find a lot of rest
with all the many cat stands
they are living at their best.

Everyone is pleased with our home
it is everything we want and need,
we can go for walks in the woods
and let all our dogs take the lead.

I only wish that my parents
could have seen our latest place,
but since they left this earth
that just isn't the case.

I know that they are Angels
who watch over all of us here,
their love and protection
is always very near.

I pray that one day
when our time on earth is done,
we will meet at the bridge
that will be a lot of fun.

We want to live in Heaven
like the home we have here,
only there will be no loss
and we won't live in fear.

God has been good to us
and provided us with all this space,
we have the peace around us
away from the human race.

Life in the Wetland

As the sun goes down
and birds nestle in the trees,
I can hear aquatic life
in the night breeze.

Frogs are chirping
and singing their song,
like a chorus of nightlife
as we move right along.

Then you hear the bull frog
above all the rest,
his bellow is coming
out of his chest.

Mystical fireflies
twinkle in the dark,
they show their night glow
adding that lunar spark.

Crickets join in
along with the frogs,
and lizards are hiding
under the logs.

Turtles are poking their heads
just above the water,
while they patiently wait
for the fish like the otter.

Aquatic life zooms through the reeds,
and a ripple will show,
as they get near the surface
the turtles will know.

You'll hear a slash
as the turtles will dive,
they gobble fish down
barely alive.

Off in the distance
wolves howl at the moon,
the hunt will be on
so very soon.

Nature so abundant
during the moonlight,
busy as beavers
all through the night.

Hooting in the trees
owls can be heard,
the chain of events
is not so absurd.

For each nocturnal creature
nature is fulfilled,
as morning approaches
the water is stilled.

Enticing the aquatic life below
bugs will dance on the surface,
feeding the fish
and giving them purpose.

A rustle of movement
from the edge of the brush,
mother ducks dive in the water
their ducklings will rush.

Nocturnal life becomes silent
and the daylight begins,
the turtles bask in the sun
the fish shuffle their fins.

The bright sun rises
day life joins in,
a whole world of its own
is about to begin.

A snake occasionally will skim by
emerging from the left-over fog,
as he catches his breakfast
a fat lazy frog.

The well-fed fish
sometimes jump in the air,
with their bellies full
they have not a care.

The loon is awake
as they sound off quite loud,
a creature of stature
who can be very proud.

Life in the wetland
is always in motion,
ponds, lakes and rivers
and even the ocean.

Earthly Power

Everywhere on this earth
there is energy of power,
like the life stages
you see in a flower.

If a person could watch
a flower as it grows,
it starts out from nothing
till blossoms will show.

Only with time lapsed photography
is a flowers movement of growth seen,
not possible with the naked eye
but so very amazing and keen.

The energy of power
is seen in a storm,
as the static electricity
begins to form.

The pulsating of thunder
sends blasts to the earth,
and then comes electricity
with lightning's rebirth.

As this electrical power
strikes static rays down,
the earth lights up
like a blaze all around.

Producing this kind of energy
earthly power will feed,
supplying something magnetic
that our planet will need.

Often following a storm
some rainbows will show,
another array of energy
with colors that glow.

All the varieties of weather
on this earthly plain,
are beyond fascinating
we have much to gain.

Thunder and lightning
wind, rain, and dust,
all powerful energies
are always a must.

The earthly energy
plays its own game,
how mother nature reacts
is rarely the same.

Strong winds that develop
can sound like a train,
tornadoes are powerful
and followed by rain.

So, when eagles are seen
soaring in the sky,
they remind me of storms
just passing by.

Energy builds up fast
its strength will devour,
all things in his path
with its earthly power.

Vermin

Certain wild animals
are considered fuzzy and cute,
but when they are destructive
I don't give a hoot.

I remember the one day
hubby came running in the house,
he was so thrilled to tell me
a rabbit was running all about.

He yelled excitedly
hurry come quick,
and I ran out the door
like a country hick.

He pointed towards the garage
at a big rabbit on the lawn,
I shot him a look of disgust
I thought it was a fawn.

My lack of enthusiasm
made my husband laugh,
he was so tickled
his gut nearly busted in half.

I twirled my finger in circles
up in the air,
as if to say 'big deal'
I don't really care.

Because I love all creatures
I don't like to be unkind,
then I saw just a vermin
something I didn't expect I would find.

My words to my hubby
were something like this,
I yelled yippee skippy
almost in a hiss.

Then I thought of my garden
all flattened to the ground,
with all my beautiful plants
that were all dead and brown.

I don't see cute and fluffy
I see nothing but a pest,
they are food for an eagle
at their very best.

They eat all your vegetables
and tear apart your entire garden,
people think they're cute
but I won't give them a pardon.

I say stay in the woods
away from my house,
I think I would much rather
see a damn mouse.

At least all my cats
can keep mice away,
rabbits need to live in the woods
and that is where they should stay.

They have plenty of vegetation
deep in the woods,
they don't belong in my yard
eating all my goods!

Destructive rodents is all they are
and the word cute doesn't fit,
I have no desire to see them
not even one little bit.

I thought of live trapping them
and driving them far away,
where they can't destroy everything
is all I will say.

You can take their big eyes
and that twitchy nose,
and chase them away
with the garden hose.

Rabbits become such a burden,
and multiply by the dozens,
they invade your yard and garden
with all their siblings and cousins.

Rabbits are furry wrecking balls,
and we've all had enough,
when we see all the damage
they do to our stuff.

So, you know I won't act really happy
when you come running to me,
to point your finger at a rabbit
and tell me what you see.

As far as I'm concerned
those carrot eaters are a sin,
they are the worse kind
of destructive vermin.

A Beautiful Place

By Mike Mortenson

Sometimes I forget what a beautiful place we have to live on,
and all the things that bring us joy and happiness.
To think about all the things that we have been given,
to help us make our lives better and to have comfort and rest.

This place we call earth, and all its beauty and splendor,
from the very beginning of time when God created all this,
there is nothing like it in all of the universe,
that compares with everything here, and when I leave here this I will miss.

Life is what you make it here, but think about what I have said,
so, people from all over the world, we need to come together.
Take away the hate, the hurt, and all those kinds of things,
it would be so cool if we all could do this, how beautiful that
would be, to see how much happiness to each of us it would bring.

So, if you just had a tear come to your eyes,
after reading what I just wrote,
then my friend you have a lot of love
in your heart and God sees that, I know that I can quote.

Take care my friends, whoever you may be,
I really hope that we can meet and see each other,
so that I can hug you and tell you how beautiful you really are,
not just on the outside, but on the inside too, even if you are not close,
but a long way away and so far.

To me it does not make any difference what color you are,
I just know that we are all here to help each other,
for we are all from that same place above,
we all came here to learn that one thing called love.

An Animal's Point of View

By Mike Mortenson

No matter what kind of animal they may be, each and every one has something to say. They may not talk to us like humans always do, but they communicate to us in their own special way.

Animals have great memories, if you ever helped one, you will find they never forget, but if you were ever mean to any, that my friend you may end up to regret.

Animals of all different kinds were sent here to be with us, they do things for us, they help us, they are our friends. We really need to listen to what they have to say, and they have a lot to tell us every single day.

Comfort and warmth on a cold winter's night, they want to snuggle with us and give us that delight, not to mention all the others including rats and mice. Dogs are protectors, while cats are just there, to pull things off walls, and to give you a scare.

They wake you up at all hours of the night, because they want your love, and that is so right. I wouldn't want it any other way, not to have animals, I think I would just fade away.

They give me a purpose for living, for this day, they gave me love, like they do every day. Animals of all kinds make the world go around, I love listening to all the noises they make, their own special sound.

When they live with you, each day is a treat, you never know when in their game, you will be beat. Yes they are a lot of fun, and a lot of work too, but just remember this, God gave them to you.

Parents

By Mike Mortenson

This morning I had to let the dogs out, and when they were done, I let them back in. I made some coffee to wake me up, sat myself down on the couch, reminiscing where I've been.

In my mind I went back in time, to visit my old life, to see old family members that I once knew. My mother and father and 3 brothers too, to tell them that I love you.

Sometimes things happen, that you cannot control, and you wish now, how things could have been different, if only I had known way back then, so that now I could be with those Heaven sent.

Life itself, for many of us, is hard to deal with, but for the many, it is a teacher that we must trust. I try to imagine seeing a daughter and son I never had, when they were born watching them grown, every single day into loving people, who got married way back then.

I know I would have loved them so, but all I have now is just this dream. So, if you're now reading this and you have children, love and cherish them, together you'll make a great team.

Be there for them, no matter what comes along, they are your family they are now a part of you. Listen to them for they have their own song, together in life all of you will make it through.

This is my song that I want to give to you, to help you with your life so dear. Be loving to each other and you will find, just how great life is, I hope all this you will hear.

Take care my friends, have a great day, be with your loving family. Love them with all your heart, for you have a gold mine there, to know this you're very smart!

Children

By Mike Mortenson

When they are born, they are given to us as miracles,
precious, yet gentile entities that will grow to be,
unique and yet beautiful creatures of this universe,
that will love you for who you are - you see.

From the moment that they are born, till they leave us here,
they will give so much back to you,
for they love with kindness in their hearts,
they know no wrong, they are so true.

So, if you have children, please do this for them,
cherish and love them like no other and always be there,
no matter what may come your way,
for they will love you more each and every single day.

Do everything you can for them,
don't fret or even worry,
it will all come back to you,
as this was the way it was intended to be.

As we get older and they are there with you,
be thankful that you brought them into this world,
there is no greater love than that of a child,
for they will carry on your legacy that is so true.

I leave you with this last message,
hold them in your arms and never let go,
hug them tight and let them know,
that you have and will always love them so.

My Beautiful Creature

By Mike Mortenson

Maybe you can tell me,
how do I start this story,
should it be about the now,
or, perhaps the past happiness and glory.

Of what you ask are you talking about,
that I really need to explain,
okay, I will tell you kind person,
this is about my dog, and his pain.

About 15 years ago,
this beautiful creature,
came into my life,
but this pain I now feel, I just did not know.

His name is Storm,
a beautiful male Australian Shepherd,
when we grew together,
a friendship we did form.

We did a lot of things together,
weathered all the seasons,
we both have grown older now,
I know that God has His reasons.

Storm has matured into an older one,
still he has a love for life,
I now lay with him to help feed him,
As he lies on the floor,
soon he will be walking through
Heaven's door.

I wish they could live longer,
but it's not for me to decide,
I can only help him get there,
he will no longer be at my side.

The pain is so great,
in my heart right now,
I wish I could walk with him,
but instead to him I must bow.

He has been my faithful friend
and it hurts so bad,
if there could only be another way,
then I would not be so sad.

I am going to miss you,
my loyal and loving friend,
but don't you worry Storm,
this is not the end.

For soon I will see you,
when I walk through that gate,
for then we will be together,
and that will be super great!

Tree Love

By Mike Mortenson

I wanted to write this poem about something that caught my eye,
I was in the backyard mowing the lawn, looking down and then up at the sky.
As I walked towards the house, I noticed something that made me think,
and then it hit me, this special thought came to me in a blink.

I saw two trees wrapped around each other,
one was bigger and taller, but it was wrapped by another.
The other tree was half the size of thickness, but stood as tall,
I just knew to never cut them down so they would fall.

It's a beautiful sight to see and then let your mind ponder,
that something nature is trying to tell us from that great beyonder.
That trees and other living things have no prejudice, they do not hate.
They accept each other no matter what color, or race and I think this is
really great!

Those two trees are black and white, have grown together over these years,
to see them together like this, just brings me tears.
Because it is a message from God above,
that no matter what race you are, we are here to love.

Nature is telling us about this message in her own special way,
we need to look up, to watch and pray.
To help each other no matter who you are,
even if you're from another country that is so far.

We are only here for a very short time,
trees live longer but have become friends of mine.
They give us shade when it's hot outside,
they do not travel, or go away, they never hide.

Trees are a part of God's big plan,
they are here to teach us and give us a hand.
Some are used to make us shelters, to keep us safe,
some are used for heat, in a nice home, your place.

So, when you see them now, be thankful they are here,
as they will grow bigger each coming year.
To me, they are now family because they have been with us that long,
this is why I dedicate the poem to them, and this is my song.

Just thanking God, for what He has done.

Open Letter to a friend

By Mike Mortenson

Dear friend, at least once in our lives, love touches us. It lasts forever. I believe that the heart goes on loving. I am therefore asking that your love and your hearts reach out to each other and embrace that very foundation of life. The world today may not be a perfect place to be, but if you really try and look really hard, you will find there really is beauty that is all around us, if you would only open up yourselves and embrace that beauty and each other. It is really all we have left to get us by and hold on to. "Once love touches us in this life, our hearts really do go on - forever."

www.ingramcontent.com/pod-product-compliance
Lightning Source LLC
Chambersburg PA
CBHW051732090426
42738CB00010B/2223